Oneness Bless
Jim O'Neill

The last force found is the 1ST Force of Energy.

A ripple of frictionless energy is everywhere.

Frictionless Love emitted by the Union of Opposites.

Publisher: James O'Neill

Other self-published Poetry book

Oneness – 2016 (Out of print)

Cover Design & Book Layout by

Fox Assoiates • Hull, MA

Printed by DiggyPOD • Tecumseh, MI

Email yourdoryman@comcast.net

5th

FORCE

is

LOVE

Acknowledge

I must acknowledge the great influence on my life by the Xaverian Brothers, my Spiritual Advisors, and my immediate family. I live in the Shining Fishing Village because my Venus, Faith H Waltman, wants me to live here.

I could not function without the services of two librarians, Kailin E Norton, and Brigid Lengyel. Also, I appreciate the loving care I receive in social services from Elder Affairs under director, Nancy Lafauce, her staff, and volunteers, who render to me their love, their empathy, and their compassion. Less I forget, Cohasset Social League has been very generous to me during the Commonwealth order to stay in place during Covid-19 Pandemic. To all living in this Shinning Fishing Village. Thank you.

The intellectual talent in the Shinning Fishing Village amazes me. All members of the Shinning Fishing Village Men's Group have at least one higher educational degree. David Bigley, Steve Devaney, and Kevin O'Connor among 10 to 12 other men have encourage me to publish this book, 5th Force is Love. To all, I thank you.

Later in 2018, I was in a class with aspiring authors. My PTSD kicked in and I became extremely angry. Dr. Sullivan, a school counselor, pointed out that I had PTSD. Of course, I denied it. The next morning, I realized two things: 1) I had PTSD and 2) I had to write about my disorder. Thank you, Dr. Sullivan, for a diagnose that has given me reason to survive 4 months or more in lockdown.

DEDICATION

To those suffering from PTSD, post-traumatic stress disorder

May my insights into my PTSD disorder be helpful to you.

I service and love others, when I live in the present moment,

When I am right, I live in my mind, and I scare people.

5<u>th</u> <u>Force is Love</u> is about living a full life of love.

When we breathe, we are alive in full control.

Hateful destruction occurs living within walls.

When we hide our light in the wall of our mind,

Our light becomes a two-dimensional energy.

Be not afraid to let your light shine before mankind.

In our brokenness, be not afraid to love.

For **Love** is living in the present moment.

Loving our brokenness, we love our neighbors.

Table of Contents

Part Three: Prime Number & Free Will

EPILOGUE

INTRODUCTION

Who is my reader?

Before Jesus had his near-death experience[1], John recorded in chapter 16: Jesus said, "Unless I go away, I cannot send you an advocate who will define sin, righteousness and the judgment of nation." 5$\underline{^{th}}$ Force is Love fulfills this prophecy.

The People of God are called to form a living community of love by sharing their life, living as the Good Samaritan, by neither telling people what to do, nor by suggesting how to fix a problem. Vatican II, in 1962, mobilized the People of God to share their lives by building bridges of reconciliation and avoid building walls of separation.

It was the beautiful heart of St. John XXIII who called for the second Vatican Council and it was the beautiful mind of St Paul VI who gave the council its logical direction.

The Gospels end with the death of Jesus. He was buried at the last hour before sundown, the beginning of the sacred time of Passover. The Acts of the Apostles notes that the women found the tomb empty. However, one woman, Mary, stayed behind, looking for the body of Jesus. Mary saw a man and asked him where he had laid the body of Jesus. He said one word, "Mary."

A joyful story whelmed up in Mary's eyes and flowed down her cheeks, as Mary wrapped her arms around Jesus and buried her head into his chest. Jesus and Mary became one love within the union of Enlightenment in the Source of our Being. How long Mary stayed there, clinging to Jesus? Only those who come from the heart knows, but, eventually, she looked up into the loving eyes of Jesus. Jesus says to Mary, "Hold me no longer, but go and tell my followers that I am alive." What followed in this early history of the People of God is a social revolution and martyrdom.

---

1   The bible says that Jesus died, was buried, and rose from the dead. Thomas Aquinas writes that life is prime matter and substantial form. When death occurs, substantial form leaves prime matter. Today, we use energy for prime matter and awareness for substantial form. Death is not a cut and dry happening. In fact, death is said to occur when there is no function in the brain stem. People have died, come back, and reported that they were aware of an after-life. (See: Eben Alexander, MD, Proof of Heaven.) Jesus, the man, had the experience of Dr. Alexander... a near death experience.

Nevertheless, down through the history of humanity, there are people who believe that the Oneness is the object of their lives, and the Oneness has blessed them with power, money, and the beautiful things of this life. The rest of us are there to serve them by enjoying the trickle of wealth we receive from them. This is the Golden Idol in which humanity has created an economic system of three classes. The Haves control humanity using three tactics,

    A) Group thinking,

    B) The past is false news, and

    C) Fear of a group of people such as, Irish, Jews, Chinese, Japanese, Hispanic, etc., who will destroy the white culture.

If we are to survive as a nation, the People of God must tear down this economic wall by building bridges to a loving community, where we talk to one another, become reconciled, and share the things of this life.

5th Force is Love calls the People of God to create a loving community, by sharing the wealth of nations, becoming reconciled and living in the now, where the Oneness of Many Names exists. The People of God must follow Jesus who multiply the loaves and fishes; the Word has multiplied in us who worship in Eastern Rite and the four MECA Churches, Methodist, Episcopal, Catholic, and Anglican. We are Jesus to love as the Father, Source of our Being, loves us.

Just like the City of Mecca is sacred to Islamic people, the liturgy of the Eastern Rite and the MECA Churches are sacred to the People of God. The People of God in the liturgy confess that it is through my fault that I separate from the present time, through my fault I will remain separate from reality, and through my most grievous fault. I am a sinner because it is my choice to do three things:

    1) Escaping the present moment by living in the mind,

    2) Willing to stay in this mind, which is madness, and

    3) Acting out this madness, by fear or by anger, destroying love.

The most important part of the liturgy is that the People of God become Christ because the Word is made flesh in them. As Christ, the People of God are to love, to bless and to forgive one another as the Source of our Being love us. In this moment of love, others will say of the People of God, paraphrasing the words of Mary as she stormed into the upper room: **"I have seen Jesus! He has come back as he promised."**

Directional Babble

My Directional Babble poetry is my life study of the Oneness of Many Names, and Her three activities in our lives. Since my poetry is a study of the Source of our Being, my poems cannot be comprehended completely with one reading. Meditation and prayer are absolutely the key to understand our call to love our neighbor as we love ourselves.

Love is a gift from the source of our new direction, enlightenment, and love, the Oneness of Many Names, who gives us only one idea at a time, each and every moment of time, because logical minded people can only handle one idea at a time. Those who come from the heart, better half of humanity, knows and intuitively multi-task. This major difference is often overlooked by authority existing in churches, governmental bodies, places of work, society, in general, or the oligarchy of greed seeking to buy power, thinking humanity as male and female.

Humanity cannot fully understand the wisdom of the Oneness; they simplify creating an erroneous, destructive force into society, even within nature itself. Everyone, who knows, wants, needs, and desires the trinkets of this life, has separated themselves from the Oneness. In the end, because of this separation, their angry madness will hurt people; especially, the people they love. Living in the present moment, where the Oneness exists, is the only way to happiness.

Two authors, Eckhart Tolle, The Power of Now, and Thomas Merton, New Seeds of Contemplation, have greatly influence my life. Tolle describes the bridges and walls as living in the now or living in an apparent reality which is in the mind and is separated from the now. Merton writes about the true self and the false self. An apparent reality and the false self are the first two parts of irrational existence leading to anger and sin. A mortal sin is defined as sufficient reflection and full consent of the will first before committing the act. The medical terms for this state of being is mental illness or madness.

Tolle and Merton describe the actions in terms that we can understand the importance of reflection in terms that are simple, yet profound leading to actions that build bridges of unification or that build walls of separation. Bridge builders are angelic servants serve the needs of others, while wall builders are authoritarian Gnostic people separating themselves from the people who build bridges.

I learned from Steve May that the Hebrew alphabet's symbols indicate a number, as well as a letter. Other languages[2] alphabets indicate only letters. Languages without the meaning of Mathematics are just babble because we have separated the logic from the inspired word. Nevertheless, Christian Scripture puts the two together in John Gospel:

In the beginning is the word.

The word is with God.

The word is God. (John: 1,1)

The word in Greek is logo or logic. When we remove logic from our language, we remove mathematics and science from the concept contained in the revealed word. These inspired concepts are the basic truths. Ed Witten uses the concept of Jacob's ladder as the starting concept of his mathematical explaining his M Theory of what happens when the Big Bang occurred. M stands for Membrane. Witten calls the energy, a Brane Notice that the word BRANE comes from Membrane. This follows the teaching in Theology that we are made to the image and likeness of God. Ed Witten is my nominee for the Nobel Prize for Ed Witten describes the theory of everything that eluded Albert Einstein.

The true meaning of The Tower of Babel is the separation of the logical languages of mathematics from Sacred Scripture inspired word. This simplify the complexity contained in Sacred Scriptures. Meanwhile, we misplace the logic of Hebrew and we forget the language of the Word. Humanity, then, can deny the logic of scripture. In this action of denial, humanity can deny the logical work of scientists.

Moreover, this denial of the logic in scripture, rewards ministers of the word the freedom to interpret the inspired words in ways that benefit the few winners over the many losers. Ministers also can declare a list of beliefs in doctrine and dogmas declaring who is righteous and who is a sinner. Minister of the word can state the importance of knowledge as being God-like. Nations under authoritarian rulers can reward and punish the faithful by their divine right as authoritarian rulers. History records that, when these things occur, the four horses of the Apocalypse ride.

---

2   Latin used by the MECA Churches uses the same symbol for letters and numbers. Latin is not the living changing language in common use in today society. It is the living changing languages that speak in babble.

5ᵗʰ Force is Love

The first shall be last and the last shall be first. Also, when we look for something it is always the last place we look. The juxtaposition is so obvious that the avoiding the logic of numbers hid the obvious that is desired by all; even those who have separated from the present moment from the starting force of everything, the 1ˢᵗ Force, Love, generated by the forceful attraction of opposites. Love is the field that is everywhere, and we move through without friction. It is the 5ᵗʰ Force found by experimental science in 2013 and one hundred years after the greatest mind, Albert Einstein, greatest productive year, 1913, received the Nobel Prize not for the theory of relativity but for particle physics when he wrote that force of photons, light particles, expanded at the square of the speed of light.

The five forces are

- 1) Gravity and the name of the particle is the graviton.
- 2) Electromagnet force and a photon is the particle.
- 3) Strong force in the nucleus of an atom with a gluon being the particle
- 4) Weak force of an electron with W particle
- 5) Force of Love and the Higgs particle is the evidence for its existence.

The last shall be first. We were created in nothing, existing in what theologians called, Purgatory. The logical creation of nothing or Purgatory is free will. Free will allows us to choose the prime maker of our being or a prime doer who reward is wealth, power, and beauty. Free will is the philosophical and theological explanation of our existence on this planet. The choice is ours: wealth, power and beautiful women or the Oneness.

Prime Number & Free Will is a discussion of developing the importance of the heart in ruling society. Remember the Field of our 1ˢᵗ Force, Love, a.k.a. the Higgs Field, is working in our lives. The evident of the ends of time is there, and we must acknowledge the prophesy contained in Revelation about the end of time and the place of the woman with twelve stars under her feet and her children defeating the fiery dragon.

Lastly, for the reader to understand the terms, mind and heart, streaming though my writings, I highly recommend that the reader view these two CDs as an example of the meaning of mind and heart, The Beautiful Mind, The Man who Touched INFINITY and a third CD, Break Through, for a near death experience.

Part One

Existing

In

Purgatory

1. Jim's Life Journey

My journey began in 1951
At the Xaverian Brothers Novitiate.
Wednesdays we went for a long walk.

On one of these walks a War Veteran
Asked: "What is life without a wife,
And a home without a family?"

Then. the Veteran laughed.
His laughter haunts me today,
Even more than the question.

I questioned the Catholic Church walls,
But my idealism dramatically ends
At a Cursillo when I was sent home.

I was totally insane.
Two Psychiatrists treated me.
The second doctor recommended

Shock treatment and medicine.
I questioned the treatment.
My Psychiatrist said

"This treatment would help
Me forget the Cursillo."
Yes, the mind does forget.

The brain never forgives.
A hidden overwhelming anger remains.
A hidden disorder stays with in me

A Post Traumatic Stress Disorder
Stays from a sexual encounter
That happened at the Cursillo.

I am the most dangerous man.
I could kill without reason.
Reason wiped from memory.

During this time in my life,
Vatican Council II happened,
And after five years of recovery,

I wanted to teach again.
The Oneness closed a window
But She opened wide a door.

The door that opened was to teach
At Xavier High School, Middletown, CT.
Brother Bob needed help teaching a course,

Introduction to Physical Science
Brother Bob classes contained
Over 35 students in each class.

At Xavier High School. I learned
My walls of righteousness were wrong,
But It is alright to be wrong. Why?

It is the hardest thing to admit. But
The Oneness always speaks
To us through the voices of others.

Without a wife, the mind will build walls,
Of separation, fearing and hating others.
The heart will build bridges of unification.

We have free will and the decision
Is the always the same in Purgatory.
Do I build walls or build bridges?

A Xaverian Brother taught
Vocabulary by comparing words
With the same meaning used differently.

Two examples are:
1) Calamity and catastrophe
2) Complete and finish.

Calamity refer to a person,
Namely, Calamity Jane,
While catastrophe refers

To a dramatic event, like
The Johnstown flood catastrophe.
The difference in complete and finish

Can be explained using heart and mind.
It is the heart see clearly, while
Everything is invisible to the mind.

Buddha uses two terms
Yin is a person who lives in the heart.
Yang is a person who lives in the mind.

The Yin goes to the heart first
Before going to logic.
All Yang learn love

By going beyond the mind
to the mind's heart, allowing
The Yang to love others.

Living in the heart or mind,
Refers to either a man or a woman.
This union of opposites radiate love.

The heart is either a left-handed man
Or a woman who multi-task.
The mind is logical men and woman

Who can only do one thing at a time.
The mind listen, hears, and enlightens
The heart in present time.

Love, live, and evil differ in spelling
By the vowels, "o" and "i".
Courage and love lie in the heart.

Fear and anger lie in the mind.
This is reason why the mind must go
Beyond the mind's logic to the heart.

Heart completes the mind.
When the mind completes the heart,
The mind is finished.

The heart finds another heart
Completing the mind.
The mind is completely, finished.

I am a Yang, who lived in my mind,
I ruled by fear and anger.
And I controlled others.

When I live in my mind,
I could kill without reason,
I am evil. I am a DEVIL

Today, my journey continues.
I breathe because breathing is life.
I live completely in the NOW.

I was called to write about spirituality.
The spiritual message of the Founders
Is absents from our day to day dialogue.

I have expanded their meaning.
I have recounted reasons why
We are in **The Age of LOVE.**

2. What is Life?

Birth
Purgatory
Building walls

Of separation
Wall builders
Rewarded

Building bridges
Of unification
Death

Judgment
Bridges builders
Rewarded

This is all
There is to life
Without a wife

Or home
Without
A family.

3. Called by Name[3]

I hated being called a Dory Man.
My friends recognized I am a Thinker,
But my Father named my job and craft.

Sharping that saw is tedious work.
Stroke on each tooth is in different direction.
My Dad had built a stand to hold that saw.

Not wanting to lose his concentration,
He needs me to do something.
I ask, "Dad, do I have to do that?"

"You're a Dory Man." My dad said.
He calls me by name, and I am his.
I was puzzled, "Dad, what's the Dory Man?"

"In Newfoundland, we have a three-man Dory.
In the Dory are two oarsmen and a Dory Man.
The oarsmen do all the work, rowing.

The Dory Man sits in the back,
Goes along for the ride.
While the two oarsmen work at rowing."

I am a true Dory Man.
The name that fits me well,
For I like to sit back.

I do observe. I gather information.
I keep straight the Dory. I correct the course.
I look at strange things, which appear unrelated.

I am a Dory Man. Just like,
The Oneness, is your Dory Man,
In all your loving relationships.

---

3   The second poem found in my book, Oneness

4. Twoness Before Time

Opposites embrace in the stillness of timeless now.
A forceful attraction of Enlightenment within Knowledge
Emits the First Force, Love penetrating our Dark Side.

The Force of Love is with us, whether we care or not.
It is a field that proceeds us and is in us. Even without
Our permission! Our existence depends on this Force.

The choice is ours alone because we have free will.
The Oneness always asks, "Whom Shall I send?"
Do we avow? "Send me!" Or do we opt for memory?

For memory leads to building walls of separation.
Stating, "Send me!" We build bridges of unification,
For we have free will in this place called purgatory.

Free choice is ours alone, where
Wall builders are rewarded in this life,
And bridge builders are rewarded in the next.

Bridge builders are made in the image of the Oneness.
Where logic is embraced by intuition, and
Love is plentiful and Godlike in them. While

Wall builders' loyalty are rewarded with earthly things.
Bridge builders unite logic within intuition, and
They are the meek to whom the Oneness speaks, for

The timeless Oneness embrace their logic and intuition.
Opposites are united in the First Force, Love, as
This Force of Love penetrates their Dark Side.

5. Living in 1st Force Love

We are the image and likeness of Oneness.
The logical mind is attracted to and within
The beautiful heart who has intuition.

Humanity must recognize the dignity
Of the person living in marriage.
Or in other relationships, such as,

Living together, gay, lesbian, or incest unions.
Love emanates from union of opposites.
Logic with Knowledge unites all as one.

Relationship is a union where
Knowledge knows, and logic listen.
This love relationship always happens,

Where the beautiful heart knows, and in
The now, the mind enlightens the heart,
On hearing the words of the heart.

The mind meditates on the pain of the heart.
Oneness will speak to the mind's heart,
Because the Oneness wants to speak.

6. Sacricide[4]

In Numbers, Yahweh said to Mariam:
"I speak to Moses because I want to speak."
We know the Oneness wants to speak.

Yes, the Oneness wants to speak, but...
Are you ready to hear and to listen?
Her words are in the secret of your heart.

However, we were given free will.
We can decide to stay in the mind.
Where we are the Lord and Master.

Our logic lies in half our brain, but logic
Neither hear, nor listen to the heart.
Logic will angerly destroy the sacred.

An example of this is the gift of a President, who
Destroys the safeguards of the Founding Fathers.
Unlike Truman, the buck never stops at his desk.

President Trump believes in the Authoritarism.
The President has placed the economy over our health.
Because his election is his most important objective.

He has violated the Sacred Rights of "We, the People."
He is a right-handed President, who has no regards
For our Sacred Rights for life, liberty, and happiness,

The President's economic cost is our sacred right to life.
The President neither cares if we die in loneliness,
Nor does the President care if we mourn for our dead.

---

4   Sacricide means, killing of the sacred. See The First Conspiracy,
     Meltzer & Mensch, pp 26

7. Let There Be Light

When life energy formed in the Higgs field
Or in the 1st Force, Love, which emanates
From the union of the Word within Knowledge,

This forceful attraction enlightens the darkness.
When LOVE'S energy bursts from the Oneness.
A forceful energy bursts forth into the darkness.

We feel it before we see it,
In loving young couple.
We see their puppy love

Higgs field or Love penetrates emptiness,
And the ONENESS LOVE ACTIVITY
Emanates from the Timeless Now

Three activities of the Oneness are:
SOURCE OF BEING, ENLIGHTMENT, AND LOVE
existing before time and space existed.

It is in this Love that we were created.
It is in this Love that we are loved
By the Oneness of Many Names.

8. Timeless

"I AM" exist Alone
Without time or space
Without beginning or end

Alpha and Omega of life
Prime Mover and Prime Doer
Existing before creation of time.

Time is a creation dimension.
A continuum existing throughout space.
Our existence is in the NOW of the Oneness.

Babble cannot describe this state.
We have never lived without time.
Separation from the now only exist in memory.

Our existence started when
Energy is placed in the created vacuum
From a place without time

A place where there is only NOW,
In a Presence existing before time.
Our existence depends this Presence.

Living in the present moment
In the field described by Peter Higgs
Love exist always in Now.

Love is our call of ministry.
Love the Oneness and our Neighbor,
Because the Oneness always Loves us.

9. Memory

While we exist in the now.
We remember past time
The past exists as stored energy

The past exists in two dimensions.
Our words become babble
Remembering the past existence.

We exist in an apparent reality,
In a false self, or in our Satanic self,
Where our Dark Energy exists.

We exist like a ship in a Bottle,
Where the Oneness' Love holds
Only the bottle in existence.

The bottle's glass separates
The ship in the bottle
From the Love of the Oneness

Separation from NOW is our first sin,
Where time stands still, EXISTING
DIFFERENTLY FROM THE ONEINESS.

10. Creation

Order of creation proceeded slowly
With the creation of what science call strings
Or St Paul named nine choir of angels.

Nine strings to be exact were
Created in the Higgs field,
Love coming from the Oneness.

Apparent reality exists in our brains
As we read in Buddha's writings,
Or the words of sacred writers.

Buddha was the first to describe
The importance of living in the Now.
Buddha believed we are changing phases.

Of the Oneness only when we exist in Now.
Pantheism is the name of this Theology.
Pantheism became Buddha babble in his day.

However, we are created in four dimensions.
We are separate from, but we are in, the 1st Force.
We are created nothingness; it is called Panentheism[5].

Other holy men were inspired.
Their inspired words were recorded,
Because their inspired words rang true.

Their stories about the Oneness' Love
These sacred writings of nations
Became the Oneness words

---

5   There is a difference between Pantheism and Panentheism. Buddha said that we are all part of God or we
     are Pantheist. However, we are separated from the love of God by Higgs Particles which happened before
     the Big bang. We exist in the Love of God but dimension or Higgs Boson separates from the Love of God.
     We are not Part of God, but we are in the Love of God or we are Panentheists.

11. Scientific Symmetry

Everything stems from Oneness.
After the Oneness created a dimension
A dimension we call the Higgs boson.

This boson contains no life energy
But it separates life energy from the Oneness.
Second Higgs boson creates empty space.

In this empty space, energy is placed.
In a two-dimensional vacuole, the Oneness
Creates energy in a field of nothing.

Spirituality of Panentheism is the norm.
Jesus said, "Heaven and earth will disappear.
The Oneness WORDS will not disappear."

The Higgs boson will disappear,
When all matter disappears into energy, where
We become Pantheist, existing in the Oneness.

Panentheism is where we exist in purgatory,
Where we build walls of separation,
Or we build bridges of unification.

When the walls of the Higgs Boson disappear,
We either remain in darkness separated by
Our created walls, or we enter the Promised Land.

Part Two:

Creation
of
Purgatory

12. Theory of Everything

With creation of the first Higgs boson.
Separation from the Oneness happens[6].
The birth of the continuum of time occurs.

In the eighth dimension when there were
Seven strings or seven choirs of Angels,
The Oneness allows Her creation, free choice.

This changed everything when the choice
Was either themselves existing in the darkness,
Or living in the source of their creation.

Thus, when everything settled down, we live
In Purgatory with free will, and at times of
Every prime number[7] we are given the choice.

A choice is ever changing,
But it is always the same choice.
Choosing either ourselves or the Oneness,

Where we either build walls
Of separation, or we build bridges
Of unification where we serve others.

---

6   Time starts with the Big Bang.

7   A prime number is the only that is multiply by ONE. At these times of a prime number we are all faced
     with the choose of the Oneness or Ourselves. We build bridges through others to the Oneness or we
     separate from the NOW by going to our mind where the Oneness does not exist. This separation from the
     Oneness occurred when we dressed in the Higgs Boson, our original sin.

13. Oneness' Play Toys

Creation starts with the Adam Particle.
The spin is either clockwise or ante-clockwise.
The spin stops as the Love Field collapses.

The pressure of the Love Field causes
The Adam Particle to break into pieces.
The pieces take on dimensions or clothing.

The dimensions or clothing separate the particles
From the Field of Love. This is known as
Panentheism or $(a + b) (0) = a (0)$

Pantheism occurs after death, when
The dimensions or clothing disappears,
Our Gloried Body is in the field or $(a + b) = a$

Our Glorified Body is in the NOW.
Our existence is within the NOWNESS
Of the Oneness of Many Names.

Death is the passage into the Oneness
A metamorphosis where we were separated
Into a Pantheism where we enjoy our glory.

Some has had a near death experience.
They have reported that a place exists,
It is desirable and glorious.

Believe it or not Jesus had
The same experience of
A near death experience.

"Destroy this temple and I will raise
It up in three days." And Mary said:
"I've seen the Lord. He is risen."

14. Order from Chaos

Second Law

Theory of everything happens
In the present moment, or Timeless Now,
Where energy exists in a vacuole.

Third Law:

All created energy exists
in one more dimension
then its dimensional energy.

Conclusion:

Humanity is living
In a four dimensional
Material universe.

The four dimensions are:
1) back and forth,
2) side to side,
3) up and down, and
4) NOW or time continuum

Living inward is Evil
Where time stands still.
In this land of Purgatory.

We must look up
To the Source of Being
To emerge from Purgatory.

15. Living in NOW

We exist in the Timeless Comer or NOW.
Oneness is the Prime Maker and the Prime Doer
And the Oneness is the Subject and Object of all love.

Oneness creates a vacuole in the First
Force. Love. produced by the embrace
Of Enlightenment within Knowledge.

Loop and string energy are placed in vacuole
Of this Field of Love. This energy field contains
Everything created, starting with the first dimension.

Thus, all phases of mass
(plasma, gases, liquids, and solids)
Is in the Oneness.

However, creation is not
Different phases of the Oneness
Or, Pantheism, as taught by Buddha.

Nor are we the Oneness
Because the second law of creation
Where we were created out of nothing.

Moreover, at the same time
the fourth law of creation
Came into existence.

No two things exist in the same
Place, at the same time. Why?
Because we were created in nothingness.

16. Examining Cosmology

Albert Einstein looked for the
Theory of Everything, a lifetime
Search, but he was never found it.

We found the Theory of Everything.
The long search was over, but then,
It got more complicated.

Theoretical scientists found
NINE types of string energy
Contained in TEN dimensions.

So far so good.
But after World War II
Japanese[8] scientist claimed that

Our created energy is
A loop string of energy.
And confusing babble reign.

String and loop theories
Compete for the
Theory of Everything.

---

8   Yoichiru Nambu

17. Adam Particle

Authors Mandelbrot, Fractal Geometry, and Wolfram,
A New Kind of Science, proved this statement.
"Complexity come from a simple repeated law."

These laws are found in sacred writings.
The Oneness laws are conceptualized and
Repeated over and over changing humanity history.

The concept missing from the theory of everything
Is the Priest Creation story of Adam and Eve.
The missing component of the theory, the Adam Particle.

From the Priest Creation story, Adam
Was asleep when God takes a rib.
From Adam rib God create Eve.

Then, a choice is made and Adam and Eve dress.
God comes into the garden and finds them dressed.
Adam and Eve are thrown out of the Garden.

Characteristic properties of the Adam Particle
From biblical concept are: The Adam Particle is
Motionless. breaks into particles being under pressure.

Force of the field collapsing, Adam particles dressed.
What did the Adam and Eve particle use to dress?
The particles dressed in the dust of broken Adam particles.

The dust formed the Higgs Bosons or dimensions,
The dimensions protected the Adam and Eve particles
From the pressure of evil[9] energy on the first field.

Coronavirus is an example of the Adam particle dressed.
In that coronavirus is dressed in a layer of fat.
Evil energy entered the field of the Force of Love.

A vacuole is created when the Adam particle dresses.
Scriptures law is repeated down history until today.
It is not good for man to be alone (without love).

9   Evil means we are living inward and we separate from the NOW

The scripture laws must be obeyed for good order.
Dissonance occurs when humanity lives without love.
The concept, it is not good for man to be alone,

Give rise to a self-loving humanity searching for love.
This is a humanity searching, demanding loyalty, and
Needing abnormal recognition thinking he is God-like.

This is not the end of the story. Jesus said:
"Heaven and earth will disappear,
But my words will not."

The law of attraction formed the galaxies.
This same law will cause heaven and earth
To vanish. It is already in motion.

The whole universe is expanding. However,
One galaxy is going in a different direction.
It is bigger galaxy than our Milky Way.

Andromeda Galaxy is the only galaxy
That is moving in our direction, and
It is on a collision course with our galaxy.

It is moving at us at the speed of light.
The fundamental laws of attraction
Makes the edge of two galaxies unite.

If Andromeda revolution is counter to our galaxy,
And when the outer edge of the galaxies meets,
The stars will appear to fall from the heavens.

Massive comets, asteroids, and even planets
Of the two galaxies with opposite spin collide,
A Big Bang occurs as we disappear into the Oneness.

We can use the Hubble telescope to see if Jesus
Is correct that there is a difference in revolution.
A collision will cause both galaxies to disappear.

18. Free Will

The complication picture gets more complicated
I have left out free will and the mathematical
Discovery of free will is the Grassmann numbers.[10]

Again, to reiterate the theory,
There were seven strings of different dimensions
Existing in space containing one more dimension.

Thus. each string exists in a reality where
The reality is one more dimension
Than the number of strings dimensions.

In the eighth dimension the strings were given
Free Will. A choice between the Oneness
Or living in the past where nothing changes.

Time stands still, fearing of the future.
The false past exists broken in memory.
It is a gift of living inward that cannot be fulfilled.

With Free Will we freely choose
To live forward in the light
Or live inward without light.

Living in the present where the
Oneness exist or living in the past,
By building bridges or building walls.

Choosing to live inward we deny growth.
Growth means change. President Trump sells
present time, while denying change and growth.

"Be not afraid," is the angelic refrain.
"Be not afraid." Is Jesus' words.
Change for the good is happening.

---

10 Grassmann said that in the eight dimension that the seven different dimensional strings turn inward and rejected living in the Now.

19. The Past

THE PAST CAN NEVER BE RE-CREATED.
The Past is shattered like glass into many parts.
Not all parts exist in the many minds that recall it.

Creating the past is a jigsaw of ideas
Presented as truths by the observer.
Ideas are always different to observers.

As much as we want it to happen...
We can never recreate the past.
We are not gods; yet a few need a master.

An Alabama Judge wants to dump all amendments
To the Constitution of the United States.
This Judge believes he won the 2018 senatorial election.

An advisor from Virginia, a friend of
President Donald J. Trump, wants to
Get back to the founder's constitution.

Many believe in white supremacy.
They believe that the black women's' vote stole
The Alabama election. The Judge is their Senator.

We are headed for a 2nd Civil War, unless
The nation heart, the Hearts who knows
are elected replacing congressional gridlock.

The choice was ours, keep the logjam.
Elect left-handed men, multi-tasking women,
Or a person who has gone to the heart as a leader.

Even if we elect of nation heart, the nation mind[11]
Believe the election was stolen by the nation heart. Then,
The Four Horses of the Apocalypse will ride.

---

11 President Trump believe that the election is set up to steal the election from him.

20. Four Horseman Riding

"Now hear this! Now hear this!
This is your President talking!
This election of 2020 is great scam.

I did not lose the election!
It was stolen from me!
By fraudulent mail-in-ballots.

Mail-in-Votes allowed by the Democrat.
This is a fraud, a miscarriage of Justice.
I am not leaving the White House

I did not lose The election:
It was stolen from me.
Attorney General Barr will defend me,

Using Federal Law Enforcement unit.
Units used in Portland, OR. It is
My duty to enforce law and order.

Joe Biden stuffed the ballet boxes.
As Lazy Joe has done all his life.
I am still your elected President."

This is a tactic that Trump often uses.
He will not go gently into the night.
We need the largest margin in history,

To defeat this President, who believes
In the Divine Right of Authority,
"Every Vote Matters" in this election

21. SHE-DEVIL

A logical man can be evil, needs power and money.
He lives in-ward reversing the word live to EVIL.
A totally evil man is "of evil," D'EVIL, or the devil.

Logical woman, wanting the same, is worse than a man.
Evil woman lives full of hatred and anger. She is a
She-Devil and she appears to have seven heads.

A She-Devil when losing will change the topics.
Often as much as seven times until she wins.
You are fighting against a woman with seven heads

Logical Barbara Bush was called the Enforcer by her family.
Logical Hillary Clinton is brilliant but lack empathy.
KimYo-jong, sister of Kim Jong Um is also logical

She has come of age and is in controls of the Army,
With an arsenal which includes the atomic bomb, but
More importantly she has the means to deliver the bomb.

The United States is distracted. BE WARN
AMERICA. *North Korea is rattling the flames*
Of war. Destruction could occur at any time.

22. Life in Purgatory

Loving self is living inward, in our head,
Where our light is in the darkness of hatred.
It is a place where nothing moves forward.

Living in our head is our original sin. While living
In the Oneness is going forward into the light,
Where we freely choose life, growth, and change.

Choose to live in a static, unchanging condition
Of a status quo is where everything stays the same.
Nothing will change unless authority approves.

Spirituality is living in the First Force, Love,
Where time and free will were created
By the Forceful Attraction of Opposite.

Our choice is living in the NOW.
It goes against status quo of
Apparent, false self, reality.

Apparent reality is where one lives
In the past, or desires future events.
It is living in our mind of anger and hatred.

I lived in this False Self of Merton.
I thought I was living in present time.
I was in a state of anger. I did not care.

My mind was like a Ship in a Bottle,
Where I controlled everything.
But I ignored everything else.

This ignorance leads to destruction,
Where this Dark Energy of anger
Rips the Field of Love apart.

This Dark Energy causes chaotic
Change that will live in our memory
And long for as the good old days.

23. Dark Energy

Dark energy gives rise to
The seven deadly sins,
It is inward thinking, and gives

Power over those living in the light.
This energy neither feel their neighbors' pain,
Nor do they share their neighbors' love.

They are the Haves owning earthly things.
These Haves obtain wealth, power, and sex
By separating themselves from the light.

They create a class of Have Nots.
The Haves claim the Have Nots
Are fat. Lazy, and envious of them.

The Haves have created a third economic class,
The Want to Have who chase an American dream.
The national debt is placed on them.

The Want to Have are taxed to pay
For the trickled economic system of greed
Where the major tax deduction goes to the Haves.

This will eventually cause the seven sin,
Anger in "The Want to Haves",
And our democracy will be in a Civil War.

A national revolt with the four Horses riding
Destruction of our nation will happen.
This is the present state of our nation.

Howard Zinn said in the Camden 26 trial,
"Civil disobedience is at the center of
American democratic philosophy."

24. Primordial State

Loop strings and anti-loop strings
Were created in the Higgs Field or
Love emanating from the Union of Opposites

Loops and anti-loops were called
Quarks and anti-quarks
Named by Murray Gill-Mann

Anti-quarks' spin is
180 degrees different
From quarks

When quark and anti-quark explode
Leaving radiating energy and particles
We call this explosion, the Big Bang

Energy and mass cools to states
Of plasma, gases, liquids, and solids
Over two hundred particles are formed

Under the right condition
Of temperature, pressure, and mass
Life occurred on earth

Eventually evolved into
Plants and animals of today
Everything is a changing.

There were seven major changes,
Recorded in the layers of the earth.
The present state is the eighth change

Scientists observed the Einstein ripple of energy,[12]
Transforming our social attitudes towards others.
Artist will record this social distancing changes.

---

12 See Back Cover

Part Three:

Prime Number
&
Free Will

25. Talking Babble

Genesis starts with the seven-day creation story.
Then, there is the creation of Adam and Eve story.
Professor Susskind[13] said these biblical stories are:

"The Fairy Tales of Hebrew Scriptures."
I look for scientific evidence of both
The seven-day creation and priest story.

I remember Yahweh asks to Job, "Were
You around when I made the world?"
Just maybe, Professor Susskind is wrong?

This is a puzzle in need of a solution.
We must look at the Union of Opposite,
Occurring in us and in our relationships

Twoness evidence occurred in nature.
When energy producing cells[14] lives a
Symbolic relation within our cells.

These powerhouse cells are passed on to us
Through the eggs of the female, benefiting us,
Like Enlightenment with the Source of Being,

Historical creation, growth, and change
Occurs naturally within the universe story
Where everything falls like Jericho's walls.

---

13 Lenard Susskind is a theoretical physicist teaching at Stanford University when he wrote this statement.

14 The powerhouse cells, called mitochondria, exist a symbiotic relationship in the female's eggs.

26. Greek Mythology

In Greek mythology, nine muses
Are created through the union
Of Zeus and the Goddess of Memory.

Later, St Paul announced
The nine choir of angels, and there
Are the nine strings in the string theory.

In 1970 a personality study
Called the Enneagram was written.
It is based on a triad of

Thinking, Intuition and Feeling.
The triad gives rise to
Nine personalities.

In the Language of the Oneness,
All intuitive knowledge handed down to us.
In the language of the Oneness is mathematics.

Nine is important for our enlightenment,
For man's enlightenment is only gained
Through intuition and experimentation.

Eighteen is another interesting number.
Enneagram create nine personalities
But male and female are different.

Most females come from the heart
And most males are logical. We are
Created to the image of the Twoness.

There are Eighteen different
Personalities of human beings
Whose union imitate the Twoness.

27. Intuitive Enlightenment

Edward Witten noticed Jacob's Ladder.
It is the answer to how
The Oneness communicates to us.

Energy flows from the Oneness
Down the nine strings to us,
Having nine personalities.

We exist in present a continuum of time.
The first dimension with cosmos existence,
Where we live in the Oneness's dimension.

Witten points out our love returns to the Oneness.
By the Law of attraction of opposites strings
Carrying our energy of love to the Oneness.

For the Law of Attraction to work
The string number is Eighteen - notice,
Symmetry of the language of the Oneness.

28. Intuition

The second group of strings
According to Witten is different.
In that it goes back to the Oneness.

The ends of strings must be reverse,
Because the first law of creation is
The attraction of opposites.

The attachment of the first set of strings
Is the reverse of the second set of strings,
Allowing the Force of Love to flow freely.

The opposite end hangs free in the vacuole.
Thus, we have eighteen strings.
If the strings were the same in this connection

To the Oneness, strings would reject the other,
Because strings must obey the first law of attraction.
It's the primal, ultimate, and first law in nature.

Thus, the order of communication is from the Oneness
Through an attached two-dimensional area in a membrane
To us back to a string attached to a membrane in Oneness.

This forms the circle of never-ending Love.
When the circle breaks, I is dominant as in
I know; I want; I need; I desire. I am.

I am Satan there is no other.
The choice is: I can be evil, or
I can be a servant in Love.

29. Moral Laws

Ten the number of Commandments
Given to Moses by I AM WHO AM.
First Three commandments relate to I AM.

The last Seven relate to the actions of man
Three and Seven are sacred numbers
Three and Seven are Sacred Prime Numbers

Three relates directly
to the Oneness.
Seven is sacred because

On the Seventh day that Oneness rested,
Which brings babble to the greatest gift of all
 Is Enlightenment.

Living in the Now is living in the presence
Of three activities of the Oneness.
ORIGINAL SIN is living in our mind.

30. Cyberspace War

Armageddon is happening in cyberspace
Of the mind, where feeling is denied and
Self-loving economics of Ayn Rand reign.

Rand is a she-devil with seven-heads.
Her logical writing is used to build
The three--class system of economics:

1) Haves, 2) Have nots, and 3) Want to Have.
Destruction will follow, because the four horses
Of war, famine, disease, and death are riding.

These are times of great separation
Where an on-going battle is within all of us.
It is a war for self-control, where

The one-eyed man is always King.
He will lead us to live in reality
Or in an apparent reality.

We are now faced with a choice,
Of either our true self or false self,
Of being either the satanic or angelic.

Living in an apparent reality is where
Everything stops, and nothing changes.
This is a cyberspace, and time stands still.

Choice is building walls or building bridges.
Walls that separates us into three classes,
Or bridges that lead us to the Oneness.

31. Hardest Way

The choice is ours; we can gloat in our victory.
We can revolt against the government.
Or we can pray for the nation.

To pray for the nation, we must stay in the moment.
Breathe is about the idea of Buddhists.
Breathe is about the first line in John's Gospel.

The prime number, two, is the only even number.
Two is the union of opposites. Breathe America,
Because living in the opposites is the third way.

The third way is the hardest for those,
Live in darkness of their mind's basket.
It's like living on their ship in a bottle.

The third way is the easier for those,
Who see, hear, and feel the pain
Of the heart because they have compassion.

Walls separates wall-builders from Love.
They see others as the enemy,
An enemy that must be hated.

I know hatred because I lived inward.
In this state, it is about me, myself, and I.
In this state, I am a Satanic Master.

I carry this tendency all my life.
I can deny it; it is always in me.
Using PTSD anger, I can play God.

The third way appears to be the hardest,
But it is the easiest way to unification, because
My love connects to and with the Oneness.

Thomas Merton, Guru of the 60s peace movement,
Wrote: "Catholics believe in a personal God,
Who loves them and moves God's people to love."

To change from being a Satanic Master,
We start with asking the Oneness, "Why me?"
It ends with Love, Blessing and Forgiveness.

Satanic Master decreases
When we love, bless and forgiven.
And love of serving others will increase.

At the same time,
We love our neighbor.
We love the Oneness.

The Oneness wants to speak
To us in the secret of our hearts,
Where we exist together as one.

32. Theology & Cosmology

Theology and Cosmology appears to be diametric.

Cosmology investigates the "Works of God."
Theology studies the intuitive "Word of God."

Both studies are the opposite side of a coin.
Studying one, we investigate the other.
The subject of love is the unchanging Oneness.

We do know this: opposites attract each other.
Two is a prime number, in which opposites attract,
Just as, within the all-knowing Oneness is the Word.

The Word loves the Oneness, who knows.
This love gushes forth into the vacuum of space.
We were made in this vacuum to the Oneness's image.

We know this truth through the inspired word.
We found this truth through experimentation.
Both methods describe the same field of love.

The Oneness of Many Names is the source of love.
This love emanates everywhere and is friction-less.
We are in this love. We are not the love of God.

Separation from the Oneness is by the Higgs boson.
A single Higgs Boson does not contain energy.
A vacuum is created by two Higgs Bosons.

Buddha's idea is corrected by scientific experimentation.
Buddha believed we are all facets of a changing God.
However, we are not pantheists; we are panentheists.

33. Three Big Lies

Most logical people do have empathy.
They care for their parent and their neighbor.
Neighbors cite chapter and verse of their love,

Logical people love for their neighbor,
Feel their pain, but not everyone feels
Their neighbors pain. There is Ayn Rand.

Ayn Rand's business attitude is reflected
In <u>Atlas Shrugged.</u> Her heroine denies her feelings.
Rand becomes the trickle-down economics guru.

Creating a trickle-down economics class system,
Placing the national debt on the American dream.
Trickle-down destroys this dream using Two Big Lies.

The first big lie is that compromise is a "Dirty Word."
It is not only a lie, but it also denies the bargaining
Practice used all over the world where everybody wins.

John Nash wrote three papers called, <u>Theory of Games.</u>
His papers were read by two Economic Professors[15].
They applied his theory to a real-life situation.

The three papers in Theory of Games conclusion
Was that there is a zero-sum gain in all bargaining.
Everybody wins. No one obtains more than the other.

John Nash, Mathematics Professor at Princeton U.,
Won the Nobel Prize in economics, not mathematics.
Nobel hated Mathematics and it is purposely excluded

I strongly suggested that you see the movie,
<u>The Beautiful Mind.</u>   Nash's acceptance speech
Defines love in the audience disappearance scene.

---

15   John C. Harsanyi and Reinhard Selten were co-winners in 1994

If the biggest political lie, "Compromise is a dirty term"
Is true, then the second bigger lie is, "Paying taxes is free speech."
because "Money makes the World go around.[16]"

Citizen United Decision of the Supreme Court
Lead to cooperation given the right of citizens,
allowing to tax free money for Political Action Coop.

The intended consequence of Citizens United
Is known to the Cooperation Lawyers, in which
They created a new pathway to become a citizen.

Citizens United not only does corporation
Have the rights of citizenship, but this decision allows
Millionaire becomes a citizen by applying Euclid 1st Law.

Euclid first law: "It is obvious, that things
Equal to the same thing are equal to each other."
It is so obvious that I do not waste time proving it.

The Cooperation lawyers know the 15th, 16th, and 19th
Amendments eliminated all classes in our Constitution.
Only person who has the Right to Citizenship is a citizen.

Jared Kushner offered Chinese Millionaires
The Right to Citizenship if they bought a
Condominium in Jersey City from him.

A millionaire tried to buy the Wall Street Journal.
The government said He was not a citizen.
He became a citizen three month later.

The Greatest Lie of all is an amendment is needed.
The Supreme Court's Brown Decision changed education.
Lawyers used Citizen United case to create a new pathway

To citizenship for millionaires. To change the Supreme
Court Citizen United decision, it can be argued
Using Euclid 1st Law, that all taxpayers are citizens.

---

16 A song title from the movie Carbaret

34. USA Problem

Armageddon is happening in the Near East.
Four horses of war, famine, disease, and death
Are riding; many solutions have been proposed.

It is impossible for the USA to put
Into the Near East Regular forces,
For we look like an invading army.

Our military is taxed beyond reasonableness.
Suicide and PTSD plague our Veterans.
Mental illness will be our destruction.

Our troops were placed in terrible conditions.
Left without protection, under constant stress.
They still carry on under this inhuman stress.

If I cracked under the best of conditions,
We should not be surprised when a warrior
Cracks because we did not have their six.

The writing is on the wall.
Suicide abounds from years of stress.
PSTD anger is present in our nation.

The seed of anger is festering,
Our government has failed us.
Overwhelming force is not the answer.

35. Inspiration and Sacred Scripture

The great Jewish scientists always referred
To their Hebrew scriptures to find answers
For problems that appears in nature.

Ed Witten uses Jacob ladder as the base
For his M Theory that unites
The string and loop theory together.

Grassmann numbers comes directly
From the story of the fall of Satan
And the seven choirs of angels.

The answer is in sacred scripture.
It is always in the Word of God.
Enlightenment is there for us to read.

Hebrew Scripture writes about Raphael,
Christian Scriptures mentions Gabriel and Michael.
These are Archangels with special jobs.

Michael leads other Archangels
To drive Satan out of Heaven.
Raphael guided Tobit or Tobias.

Gabriel was the Messenger
Announcing the Power from on High,
If Mary accepted, will overshadow her.

Remember once an Archangel.
Always an Archangels!
Their job is always the same.

36. Special Forces

In the Shining City Fishing Village,
Lives a Seal, who ran for U.S. Senate.
His opponent came from the Heart.

He lost to the Heart for she knew banking.
Seal job is to fight, council and announce.
As a Seal, he will always be a Seal.

For Seals are our Archangels
Having the same job as Archangels:
To fight, to guide and to announce.

Seals are the ones who will drive ISIS
Out of the Near East and will be the guide
To the Muslims fighting the darkness.

We cannot fight conventional war.
This is a battle of ideas fighting for the heart
Of a mainstream religion and our humanity.

Seals will announce the good news.
We will avoid the seeds of our destruction.
Seals are always our Archangels.

37. Live, Evil, and Love

Our life can be expressed by different words.
These words are live, evil and love.
These are the words of a life in purgatory.

Purgatory is where we are living.
This place is where evil and love exist.
The choice is reality or an apparent reality.

Oneness must be the subject of our love.
Love is a joyful activity occurring in the NOW.
Love doesn't exist in two-dimensional energy.

Our universe is four dimensional:
Back and forth, up and down, side to side, and NOW.
The first dimension is the continuum of time or NOW.

Everything is contained in one more dimension.
Memory is two dimensional, where we live inward,
Thinking about the past, while we live in the now.

Our memory is stored two-dimensional energy.
Oneness holds this energy in existence.
Oneness does not exist in past memory.

Memory is like a ship within a bottle.
The bottle's glass separates Oneness.
The ship exists in Tolle's apparent reality.

I think, I know, I want, and I desire.
These thoughts exist only in our minds.
Past is to delve into the non-existent future.

Inward ideas separate us from love.
Judgment clouds our minds.
Others become our hated enemy.

Hatred is remembering past injustice.
Tribalism, and customs destroys others.
Peace will occur when we love outwardly.

Love and peace are experiences of living.
In the Timeless Now, where Jesus does not save.
It is Intuition and Logic in the Oneness that saves.

Word in Jesus Enlightens, but does not know,
Word must be in the Oneness to know.
Only, then can the Word enlighten us.

Believing that Jesus saves is a fallacy based
On "The Word is God." It does not
Include the idea, "The Word is in God."

38. Building Bridges

Love is limiting logic to the embrace of another heart.
In the heart, compassion and empathy lie.
Love is a joyful experience of exaltation and pain.

Empathy occurs when we care to really listen.
Compassion sees pain, hears pain, and feels pain.
Compassion embraces the pain of chaos.

Love experience depends on the emotions.
Emotions are real when we feel the pain.
Emotions are necessary in loving realities.

Love does not depend on the individual's sex.
Love is friendship, courtship and becomes one,
Which denies having sex means you love me.

Embracing self-love separates us from Oneness.
Exotica is a fleeting love that is not mature.
This love is living inward and demanding love.

I think, I want, I need, I desire are paths to things,
Where trinkets are more important than people.
I am a Satanic Master when trinkets are my goal.

39. Living in Memory

Choosing trinkets is living in this purgatory.
Where Oneness' Love cannot reach.
Your ship destination is the brink of Hell.

The language of God is mathematics.
The prime numbers are when things change.
The prime number, TWO, is a union of opposites.

Change occurs when the choice is Oneness or self.
At prime number, free will has the same choice,
Where life reverse the spelling of live to evil.

80% of logical people have a mid-life crisis.
Our free will chooses between love and evil, or
Between "Why did this happen?" and "I know."

Love demands that we ask the Oneness, "Why?"
If I do not ask "Why?" Then, I am right.
Being right causes separation; evil happens.

Therefore, we live in purgatory.
This is our pot of STEW, where our choice
Is for life's trinkets or the judgment after death.

We must listen to the heart who knows.
Jesus meditated to hear the heart of the Oneness,
For Jesus said: "It is the Father that sends me."

Jesus meditated; the Word in Jesus did not know.
Jesus meditated to hear the Father who sent him.
Thus, logic must be limited to the heart of another.

Today, we must elect those who come from the heart,
Meek person who listen to the ONENESS' heart and
Hears in his heart the intuitive words of the ONENESS.

40. Meek Man

Oneness speaks when we open our hearts.
Oneness wants to speak to the quiet mind.
Oneness speaks in many types of meditation.

My Venus often meditated on these words:
Oneness comes in time, without time.
In time, no oneness is a timeless comer.

In the Hebrew Testament,
The meekest man is Moses.
The oneness spoke to him.

Moses was sent into exile by the Pharaoh.
Moses killed and overseer of the Jews.
His punishment was to die in the desert.

Moses defended a group of sisters.
He married and had children
By the strongest and oldest sister.

Mariam accused Moses.
Of marrying outside Israel tribe and
Moses' children were not circumcised.

But Moses greatest offense was that
Yahweh spoke to Moses and not to her.
Moses, Levi, and Mariam went to the Tent.

Yahweh appeared; "I speak to Moses
Because I want to!" In anger Yahweh
Struck Mariam with leprosy.

But Moses prayed for his sister.
Yahweh told Mariam to remain
outside of the tribe for seven days.

41. Sign of Contradiction

Christ's body; our body.
Christ's advocate; our advocate.
Christ's body and blood dies in us.

The Eternal Word is in our body
Whom shall I send?
Who is willing to be Christ?

Did we say? "Here we are;
Be it done according to your word."
In a MECA Church, by Jove, we did.

We said our fiat at Communion.
Christ goes away, dying in us.
Eternal Word lives in us.

The Word transforms our lives.
Righteousness and judgment changes
Nations will redefine their judgment.

For we are the coming Christ,
Because the Word is in us.
We become one in the Oneness.

The Oneness knows our new direction,
She enlightens us and loves us, and
She changes the judgments of nations.

We are the promised Christ because "The Word
Christ love emanates from us living in the Now.
Be not afraid, all people of different races,

Color of skin, wealth, customs, or religious beliefs
Or if we are Gays, Lesbians, Transgender, and Straight,
It does not matter, because, if we live in the NOW,

We are to love as the Source of our Being love us.
Be not afraid, to be the Bridge Builders, for
We are called to love and serve our neighbor.

42. Signs and Symbols

Some say spirituality and science are a crock load.
Jesus called God, his Father not his Mother.
Oneness, you say is Feminine because She knows.

There are signs in nature that deny your premise.
There is an Old Man in the Mountains.
Also, there is the Man in the Moon.

What say ye to that? I answer:
Do you know if what you are told is a myth or fact?
Did Longfellow correctly name the rider to Concord?

Who warned the Sons of Liberty's leadership?
Longfellow needed three metric feet not five.
The man named in the poem was Paul Revere,

But Dr. Samuel Prescott warned the Colonists.
On July 4th, Americans claim they are Gays.
We ride a pony; put a feather in our hats.

We claim we are member of the Macaron Club.
We proudly tell the world we belong to a Gay club.
Old man in the mountain had a great fall,

And behind every man there is a lady.
Look closer at the full moon; you will see the Lady.
When you see her, you will never see the man again.

Where to look? The lady is looking to your right.
Her hair is dark area and her face is light area.
She slightly bowing reverently to her maker.

The beautiful mind of the moon disappears
Into the embrace of the beautiful heart
Of the moon when you see the lady.

43. Purgatory on Earth

We must remember; we are in purgatory:
The message of the Oneness does not change.
Logic must listen to the wisdom of the heart.

Wisdom is the intuitive gift given
To the heart that ponders the love
Of the Word with the Source of our Being.

Wisdom is a lifetime of meekness, for
Yahweh spoke to the meekest of men.
Yahweh wanted to speak to him.

The heart from seven continents know.
Wisdom must listen to hear her voice.
Humanity must see, hear, and feel her pain.

It is a matter of social relationships.
Oneness is the prime maker in all unions,
Where the heart embraces logic.

The heart knows what is right.
Logic and the heart become one.
Not only in marriage, but also in all

Gay, lesbian, living together partnerships
Where society must respect the dignity of
Humanity, for the Oneness loves all of us.

The heart in all relationships knows like
The Source of our Being knows our direction.
Society must not make laws that is unenforceable[17].

Just as society celebrates a new union of marriage.
Society members are the sinner not the mother,
When society members suggest abortion to her.

---

17   Theologian Thomas Aquinas said we should not make laws that are unenforceable and theologian Cardinal Avery Dulles suggested abortion unenforceable. (National Catholic Reporter. Editorial, on Dolan 5/15-28/2020 pg. 16)

44. Quantum Computers

When scientist created the Quantum computers,
The creating small bits of energy is for data protection.
The data reveals we live in a more complex universe.

These small bits of energy are called entanglements.
They noticed a very complex gathering of energy
Existing throughout our four-dimensional universe.

The scientists found the complex energy disobeys
Our fundamental law existing in our universe,
The whole is equal to the sum of its parts.

This law governing the complex mass of energy is,
The whole is greater than the sum of its parts.
Two laws can only exist if two universes exist.

Entanglement explains the Ed Witten's M Theory
In which a six-dimension universe comes
In contact with a four-dimension universe.

This is the proof that Witten must be given the Nobel Prize,
Because Witten not only shows that we talk in babble, but he
Also uses the inspired word to correctly describe our universe.

It also explains metamorphic change to our bodies.
In death where our glorified body is under a new law.
It is the evidence that Pantheism occurs.

It is also the final proof that the Oneness
Is the subject of all love as Merton has claimed?
It is the reason why the mind and heart must breathe.

For it is in breathing that is are in contact
With the Source of Our Being, because,
When we breathe, we are alive in the Oneness.

45. Artists

In all tribes, cultures, and nations,
It is the artist who left, leaves. and will leave
The final message of humanity's destruction.

Records of the past have been left to humanity.
Humanity's future can investigate the past
The past indicates humanity's destiny.

Cavemen artists left pictures of their presence.
Humanity sees these records of the past that
Give humanity a glimpse into the future.

The Dead Sea Scrolls were accidentally discovered.
Scrolls that left a record of an all-knowing deity.
Record shows that man is the cause of change.

History of a mad man was left by the artists,
In the concentration camps of a fascist nation.
The contrast is there. The artists left the message.

Humanity must choose a future.
A present that will investigate the past
And knows humanity's future survival.

Satan's Angels do not know humanity's pain
Emotionless, multi-layers of separation
Lies between them and a destroyed humanity.

The Oneness is the source of a new direction,
Enlightenment and love are always the same.
Our choice is either Love or the Golden Idol.

Listen to the voices of those who feel pain.
Embrace their pain; it is the way to love.
Love is the only way we will save humanity

46. "Whom shall I send?"

Love is an experience of
Limiting logic to the embrace
Of the heart of another.

I searched for the treasure
That is more precious than gold.
I found love in the arms of his Venus.

Venus came down with leukemia.
Five years, I witnessed.
Compassion care Venus received.

The medical personnel felt her pain.
They were constant in their demeanor.
Always there for Venus and me.

My meditation was on the Word of God,
As it is contained in the Gospel of John.
I found Oneness' love in this Gospel.

The Oneness always reveals Her direction.
Revealing one idea at every moment.
My wisdom was developed over time.

My wisdom is the gift of enlightenment
Of intuitive knowledge given my heart
As I pondered the Love of the Oneness.

I write in babble because
My language does not contain
The Works of the Oneness, whose

The inspired word of the Oneness is contained in
The works of the Oneness creation, by blending
Symmetry within beauty, harmony, and consonance.

47. Love

To breathe is to live, to use our talents,
To serve, and to love one another as
The LOVE, within us, loves.

Love is NOT a noun, where we are
Rewarded by the LOVE within us, but
Love is an active relationship,

Of limiting the beautiful mind[18]
To the embrace of a beautiful heart[19],
Creating a joyful lifelong experience.

Where the beautiful mind's look,
Word, or touch calms the worry,
The anxiety, the fear of the beautiful heart.

However, when a passionate story
Overwhelms the beautiful heart's eyes
And flow down the cheeks,

The beautiful mind must embrace
And hold the beautiful heart
Until long after the flow stops.

This is the very moment, where
The mind and heart become One Love,
Within the First Field of Love.

This First Force, Love[20] emanates
From the forceful attraction of
Enlightenment in the Source of Being[21].

---

18 John Nash, The Beautiful Mind, said I am logical, but you brought me beyond logic.
19 In the secret of my Heart, God teaches wisdom. (Psalm 51: 6)
20 This refers to the Higgs Field or Holy Spirit
21 See (John: 1, 1) The Word is in God, St Thomas Aquinas Summa Theologica, Book I and Sister Lauds and Vespers, "Glory be to the Source of Being, Eternal Word and Holy Spirit."

EPILOGUE

48. Prayer of Love

O my Beloved Oneness of Many Names,
You formed our life energy in your love.
You are the source of our new direction.

You are our inspired enlightenment
And Lover within us.
We love You and we adore You.

Help us, Our Beloved Oneness,
To love You as You exist in all
Our family, our friends, and our foes.

Help us, Our Beloved Oneness,
To be the good and loving Samaritan
With everybody we meet today.

Above all, give us the strength
To recognize and ask pardon
Of those whom we have offended

Or hurt by our thoughtlessness and
Satanic greed, pride, lust, anger, envy,
Gluttony and sloth in words and deeds.

Be there for us, Our Beloved Oneness,
So that we will love, bless, and forgive
All those who hate us and despise us,

Who will condemn and inflict on us,
Mental and bodily harm because
Of our activities, and religious belief.

Unity in the Oneness of Created Newness,
Intervention and Love grant us
The wonderful gift to love You always.

Then, Our Beloved Oneness of
Many Names, do with us what
You will, for You are in all of us. Amen

49. Let us Pray

Here we are, Beloved Infinite, Timeless,
Frictionless Field of Oneness.
You ask: "Whom shall I send?"

Send us, Your Children, as Your messenger
Of love to reform broken nations, and develop
Love, joy, compassion, and empathy in nations

By collegiality, talking to each other,
By reconciliation, hearing the pain of others
And by building bridges unifying nations.

We can only do this by
Loving You for You exist in all of us.
We love You alone.

You are our Beloved Oneness
Whose kingdom, power, and glory
Will last forever. Amen

50. Jim's Sayings

Logical Babble and the Golden Rule sets standard for judging, allowing Wall Builders to be winners in this life.

Bridge Builders listen to the hurting heart and hear the word of the Oneness in THEIR hearts.

Love is the joyful experience of limiting logic to the embrace of the heart.

Wisdom is enlightenment heard in the heart when the heart ponders the joyful experience of another's love.

Sin is the separation from the Love of the Oneness.

Willing to stay separate is madness.

Enforced rights of separation are immoral acts.

Prime number is the heart's choice between either Oneness's love or claiming rights, wants, needs and desires over others.

Logical HEART is a calamity destroying the HEART's loved ones.

Non-violence love and forgiveness will save humanity.

Leadership is serving; People of the Oneness need to serve humanity.

Embrace the meek man; the Oneness speaks to him.

In all loving relationships, starts with the Oneness.

The beautiful mind of the moon disappears seeing her beautiful heart.

51. Jim's Blessings

Always, keep in mind the Force of the First Love comes from the strong attraction of the Word with God who exists in time as the Timeless Comer. Separation from the Timeless Comer is the Dark Side by living within the walls of your body.

May the Force of Love of the Word with God be with you. May you share this Force with others by **Neither** telling people the standards to live by, **Nor** telling them how to fix a problem, but share your life as the Good Samaritan as you live your life in the First Force, Love. May the First Force be always with you.

Jim O'Neill

Your Dory Man

Shinning Fishing Village

51. Jim's Reading List

Theoretical Physics

- Greene, Brian, The Fabric of the Cosmos
- Hawking, Stephen, A Brief History of Time
- Kaku, Michael, Hyperspace
- Wolfram Stephen, A New Kind of Science

Mathematics, Science and Theology

- Alexander, Eben, MD, Proof of Heaven
- Chardin, Père Teilhard de, The Phenomenon of Man
- Cho, Adrian, Science Magazine, Feb. 11, 2016
- De Mello, Anthony, Awareness
- Mandelbrot, Benoit B., The Fractal Geometry of Nature
- Nash, John F. Jr, Theory of Games
- O'Murchu, Diarmuid, M.S.C., Quantum Theology

Buddhism and Hinduism

- Hanh, Thick Nhat, Teaching on Love
- Tolle, Eckhart, The Power of NOW
- Yoganaanda. Paramhansa, The Essence of the Bhagavad Gita

Bible Studies and Love

- McKenzie, S.J, John L, The Two-Edged Sword, 1956
- Merton, Thomas, New Seeds of Contemplation
- Nolan, Albert, Jesus Today

Historical, Biography and Personalities

- Duggan, Lisa, Mean Girl, Ayn Rand, The Culture of Greed
- Gray, John, Men are from Mars, Women are from Venus
- Meltzer & Mensch, The First Conspiracy
- Nardo, Don, The Inquisition
- Thornton, John F. and Varenne, Susan B., The Essential Pope Benedict XVI
- Pierce, Herb, Power of the Enneagram
- Swalwell, Eric, Endgame
- Zinn, Howard, A People's History of the United States

CD's

- The Beautiful Mind, John F, Nash, Jr.
- The Man Who Touch Infinity, S. Ramanujan
- Break Through, 2015, a near death experience.

$10.00
ISBN 978-0-578-74023-2
51000>

9 780578 740232